Living Without Money

Why and How to Live Without Money (or at Least with a Lot Less Money)

by Geoff Vagnier

Table of Contents

Introduction 1

Chapter 1: The Dichotomy of Wealth Groups 7

Chapter 2: Understanding Minimalism and Money . 11

Chapter 3: Distinguishing Your Wants vs. Your Needs 19

Chapter 4: How to Dramatically Cut Costs 25

Chapter 5: Tips for Avoiding Temptation 37

Chapter 6: How to Make Use of Automatic Savings 41

Conclusion 45

Introduction

There's an inverse relationship between having more and needing less that dictates the quality of life a person can experience. For example, if all other variables remain static, and all of a sudden you have more of something - let's say *money* for example - then you're better off, right? And conversely, if all other variables remain static, and all of a sudden you need less money, then you're also better off. So assuming you want to be better off, it's a good objective to either increase your financial wealth, or decrease your dependency on money.

But let's take this one step further... Are these two concepts truly equal? Financially speaking, the answer would be "yes." But in terms of gaining happiness, the answer is a loud and resounding *"NO!"* Time and time again, we see people join the "rat race" and work to the bone for more money, and once they get it: firstly, it's never enough and they always want more, and secondly, it becomes a full time job just to protect what they've managed to accumulate.

Happiness is *never* achieved this way, and that's a guarantee!

So what's a much simpler, better way that can actually lead to true and lasting happiness? That's right, **needing less!** In this book, I have included everything you need to know about living on less money and adopting a minimalist mentality. So if you're ready to reduce your dependency on money, then let's get started!

© Copyright 2015 by Miafn LLC - All rights reserved.

This document is geared towards providing reliable information in regards to the topic and issue covered. The publication is sold with the idea that the publisher is not required to render accounting, officially permitted, or otherwise, qualified services. If advice is necessary, legal or professional, a practiced individual in the profession should be ordered.

- From a Declaration of Principles which was accepted and approved equally by a Committee of the American Bar Association and a Committee of Publishers and Associations.

In no way is it legal to reproduce, duplicate, or transmit any part of this document in either electronic means or in printed format. Recording of this publication is strictly prohibited and any storage of this document is not allowed unless with written permission from the publisher. All rights reserved.

The information provided herein is stated to be truthful and consistent, in that any liability, in terms of inattention or otherwise, by any usage or abuse of any policies, processes, or directions contained within is solely and completely the responsibility of the recipient reader. Under no circumstances will any legal responsibility or blame be held against the publisher for any reparation, damages, or monetary loss due to the information herein, either directly or indirectly.

Respective authors own all copyrights not held by the publisher.

The information herein is offered for informational purposes solely, and is universal as so. The presentation of the information is without contract or any type of guarantee assurance.

The trademarks that are used are without any consent, and the publication of the trademark is without permission or backing by the trademark owner. All trademarks and brands within this book are for clarifying purposes only and are the owned by the owners themselves, not affiliated with this document.

Chapter 1: The Dichotomy of Wealth Groups

As we head deeper into the 21st century, we're often inundated by two highly conflicting reports from the media—that more youngsters are joining the millionaire ranks than ever before, and that people of this age handle their finances far less responsibly than at any other point in human civilization. The ease with which things are available for purchase today, whether by way of the instant temptation of infomercials or the convenience of one-click doorstep-delivered purchases, often guarantees that having money in the bank will automatically translate to thoughtless spending at one point of time or another.

Yet, how does that explain the wide dichotomy between the groups of people reaching financial success at early ages and those who can't seem to hold on to a penny, but are instead drowning in debt? Because, at the same time, the credit card industry is enjoying numbers the likes of which have never been experienced before either.

Well, for starters, those two groups—the millionaire youngsters and the constant paupers—never entirely intersect. In fact, with the growing financial wisdom among younger generations, the basics of saving and investing are almost commonplace today—and significant sections of new wage earners are heavily capitalizing on them to insure future wealth, early retirement, and various other such financial objectives.

However, in either case, the first step is dictated by the same question — How little can you live on today to ensure that you'll have plenty in the bank tomorrow? Furthermore, because of rising inflation and the pay rise freeze in many professional sectors ever since that nasty economic meltdown of 2008-09, there are a vast numbers of people out there whose pay just can't keep up with increasing commodity prices and cost of living.

Thus, whether your purpose is to live on less than you make for the sake of survival, or for the sake of smart investing, you still have to learn to do the same thing: live with a lot less money? And that's exactly what this book is geared to help you achieve, compiled from condensed experiential wisdom of decades of earning high and living low. Trust me, it's not that difficult to do. Keep reading.

Chapter 2: Understanding Minimalism and Money

Yeah, you read it right. Saving money embraces every basic philosophy and principle embodied within the practices of minimalism. And no, minimalist living isn't something practiced by unwashed hippies living on the fringes of society. In fact, as early as 2004, minimalism has seen an en-masse movement among the central pillars of societal development—the rich and famous, the wealthy and wise, all adopting it as a measure of defense against the chaos of modern living.

Why is that? Well, as I discussed before, the advantages enjoyed by everyone in today's society are mind-bogglingly more convenient and geared towards maximum expenditure than ever before. And why wouldn't it be? After all, you spending money to buy products is the basic transaction which runs every aspect of the financial world, even affecting the money available to governments for their work. Thus, every form of media is saturated with ways to spend cash on empty conveniences, and the government's job has been reduced to ensuring that no single company or person gains enough monopoly on all their spending targets that they would be able to dictate their will on nations with impunity. Beyond that, think of the grand cycle of spending which you're stuck in.

People in older times would happily walk along dirt roads to reach centers of education and learning, or go on soul-searching trips across the world to learn more about themselves and the cultures which make up humanity as a whole. They would gain employment where needed to fuel the next leg of their trip, carry money around on their travels, sleep and eat wherever they could, and concentrated on personal development above all else. But, they didn't pay taxes, so they weren't considered as an ideal template of behavior for the future. They weren't bound by qualified regulations which told them that you needed to be recognized as a protected being under organization X, Y, or Z—and so citizenship was born. After those came about, even if you traveled, you were constantly bound by rules which would now separate humans protected under organization Y and those under organization Z, and each would be pushed to pay tithes to such entities for the protection and official recognition afforded to them. Cultures and historical backgrounds aside, each citizen would thus become a protected resource—harnessed to increase the power of this virtual organization of geo-political currency which came about as a natural evolution of tribal systems.

This system continued under the auspices of the first organizations—the nation-states and their resultant dictatorial leaderships—all the while warring on others of their ilk to build up human and material resources in order to increase the amount of money they could make as a whole, thus increasing the amount of money they could spend on their armies, infrastructure, etc. While none of these had been necessities just eight hundred years before this state of affairs came to be; for tribes at the time mostly warring for survival, food, and places to live, the new system was so entrenched into the daily lives of the people under it that it turned virtual necessities into the indisputable realities of life.

In today's world, roads and bridges are built to help people travel faster between point A and B, the former usually being their homes and the latter being offices and workspaces. Then comes the fresh new highway leading to point C, which is usually the mall or a restaurant or a movie theatre. And so, you're now stuck in a loop where you go to work for more than half your life to spend on things which usually end up at the back of a closet or stored away in the attic for half the year, all because you feel that your house would be judged by friends and neighbors if you didn't maintain a certain aura of affluence. And so, yet again, we see the virtual idea that "more stuff equals better life" so deeply deposited within the general psyche that many people regard it as an absolute and fundamental truth of the 21st century.

Furthermore, your job in all likelihood is either oriented towards generating sales, tracking sales, creating things to sell, enticing others to buy and sell, or granting others the ability to buy what they want. And so the purchases and sales which you push increase your ability to purchase things on your own, and so the cycle continues—but ultimately going nowhere at all since it's an indefinite loop. Because everyone is busy buying and selling, and then buying from others in their own time, the human existence has been reduced to the state of a perpetual hoarder. The sad fact is that even though our ancestors in older times had far less *stuff*, they were much happier with simpler blessings in life.

So here's the question—*why* do you need to buy so much stuff? What itch or wish-fulfillment drives you to believe that if you have the ability to buy everything in the world, it would lead you to any measure of happiness? Ask the richest people in the world about their money, and they would respond with utter boredom in their gaze. That's because they've already learnt the hard way that money doesn't mean much when you've alienated your family, and your friends only stick with you as long as you have moolah to dish out. Instead, money simply ends up becoming the means to an end—usually revolving around freedom from this endless cycle of earning more to spend more, or quitting their jobs to involve themselves in efforts which truly impassion them, like charities, NGOs, and other groups that dedicate themselves to improving life for others rather than feeding on their sweat and hard work.

And yet again, I can almost hear the sneers and the sarcastic whispers that they only feel this way about money because they have it. And so the cycle keeps moving on, going nowhere. Because most people have forgotten that money simply started as a way of displacing the barter system, and assigning definable and comparative values to different base commodities, which required differing amounts of effort to acquire and were necessary for life—such as goats and oranges—the idea of *currency* seems to have become the primary endgame, rather than the tool which it was designed to be. And so, humility, compassion, integrity, friendship, and other shared bonds and experiences which were believed to be the true currency of a life well lived were replaced by an arbitrarily shifting value saved in an off-shore location within a server held by your financing institution; and this is why minimalism is back on the rise.

Getting back to it, the reason why minimalism is so popular in the world of finance today is because it teaches you one *single,* but crucial, lesson—differentiating between *wants* and *needs.* Now, if you think that everything on your wish list is a necessity for happiness in your life, let me remind you of the basic principle of advertising—to drive convenience into the consumer's psyche to a point where they seem necessary for the basic existence of joy in life, essentially creating demand for a product where there was none before. So, if you feel as if your life would be incomplete without hundreds of things cluttering up your household, that's a virtual emotion created in you by the power of pushing demand—and therefore disconnected from reality.

In this book, I'll discuss ways to separate the instinct of *want* from the absolute realities of *need*. This journey won't be easy. In fact, the path you're about to undertake essentially requires *unlearning* the social conditioning via peer groups and advertising agencies which have been forced down your throat since the first moment you comprehended the sense and meaning of the idea of "possession." It's going to be the single most difficult thing you'll ever do, because the largest obstacle in your path will remain your own brain. But, in exchange, you'll gain closer bonds with family and friends, enjoy deeper experiences in everyday life, and essentially never have to feel the anxious tug of being broke ever again. Ironically, this will also lead you to a point where you will *have* plenty of money, but it will simply be laid in perspective as the arbitrary figure which it represents in the world economy—as anyone who suffered from 2008 through 2011 should readily understand—which will allow you to figure out the deeper objectives in life which truly matter to who you are as a person.

Chapter 3: Distinguishing Your Wants vs. Your Needs

As I mentioned, minimalism imparts a single lesson—figuring out the differences between what you *want* in life, and what you absolutely *need* to enjoy it. Now, as high-browed as the last chapter may have seemed, don't misunderstand me—I'm not some isolationist writing out of a hidden corner of the world where I make my own rope and hunt for my daily meal. Just like you, I can't live without the Internet, and my second weakness is good food. However, those are among five things in life which I realized form a part of my needs. I don't need a great car, a massive house, a top-of-the-line washing machine, or a gilded bathtub—but I can't do without exposure to ever evolving global knowledge, or a great meal. And I'm ready to cycle every day to ensure that even if I have a lot of money, I only work when I choose to, rather than *having* to do it to pay costly credit card bills every month.

However, I've achieved that after practicing utter austerity for a decade while working my rear off and saving every penny I could. I did that by never buying a car and having to deal with massive fuel bills even though my office was far away. I did that by only treating myself to one movie experience in a cinema every year, and even then, only if something absolutely amazing happened to be airing. I did that by never buying a TV or spending on a cable connection, catching whatever I didn't want to miss either online or by collectively gathering at a friend's house. And I did that by accepting a partner who was as fierce about financial independence as me, and who wanted a solid monetary foundation devoid of unnecessary spending as much as I did. So, in short, I gave up everything—including my own and my partner's wishes and most of my needs—for a long while, all the time working like a fanatic, to ensure that I could reach a stage where "jobs" would only involve activities which impassioned me, and where I could sustain a wholesome and healthy lifestyle replete with the few comforts which I absolutely wanted above all others, without having to work like a mule. And I could only do that because I figured out right from the start the few things which I wanted in my life above all others.

So, that's the first step for you as well. You need to sit down and figure out the things which make you tick, and the *stuff* in your life which you want only because society tells you that it's great to want to hoard the newest, shiniest, and most utterly pointless things which the corporate world deigns to offload onto consumers. Putting it simply, your basic needs are food, clothing, and shelter—that's it. Absolutely everything in which you engage yourself is an add-on, and every add-on takes a chunk out of your income to maintain itself.

Again, people might disagree vehemently with me over this, especially since I didn't include spending on friends and partners in this list. But that's because experience never shows that the best friends and partners need you to spend like a crazed monkey chucking banana peels in order to keep them close to you. They don't want or need your money, but rather your time, support, and affection. In fact, if the people around you ever make you feel like you *need* to spend on them to keep them around, kick them out. Trust me when I say that the temporary isolation till you get a proper social circle around you is *worth it* compared to finding out the true nature of your existent circle in times when you *actually* need them at your back.

Furthermore, other people I've helped in the past always objected over the point that, since I gathered at friends' places to watch a game on TV with them, they would have needed to spend on it for me to be able to enjoy that convenience. Touché. But in return, I'd invite them all for bi-monthly homemade lunches or dinners, where I would whip up great meals at low costs and teach them to do the same; give and take. And so, I met my objectives while helping them with theirs—which is what symbiotic bonds in life are all about.

In this manner, figure out the most basic part of your life which you absolutely can't do without, and then mentally exclude everything else from your "must-have" list. However, there's another catch here. While you can *somewhat* conduct this exercise and complete it halfway through by just reviewing your thought patterns, you can't use it to dispassionately understand your own spending behavior, or turn it into an actionable plan through which to live on the least possible amount of money. For that, you need to go through another exercise altogether, which I'll discuss in the next chapter.

Chapter 4: How to Dramatically Cut Costs

When you're trying to live on the least possible amount of money, the reality which you need to face and accept is that the amount of pointless spending which we do in a month is *much* higher than the amounts which actually register in our heads. And the only way to be able to see that for yourself is to fanatically record every cent you spend.

So, pick up a small notebook or diary which you can carry around on or with you—regardless of where you go—and make a note of all your daily expenses, whether normal or unusual. Everything, from your traveling fare, restaurant bills, extra soda from the vending machine, etc., needs to be rigorously recorded with absolute honesty.

Now, follow this routine for a month—day and night, even if you're coming back from a party—record every cent that you've made and spent in total within those 30 or 31 days. However, after you've followed this exercise for the entirety of the first week, it's time to sit down and take a look. We usually do this analysis at the end of the first week, and not the first day, only because the data from a single day can be highly erratic—abnormally high or low—and you don't have enough data on your spending habits through the work week as well as the weekend to make an accurate analysis yet.

Once you sit down, first just read the details of everything you spent on as well as the amounts which flowed out of your coffers. Tally up the daily totals and write them down under the relevant days. All the while, throughout this exercise, I want you to keep a figure of how much you make in a month at the forefront of your mind. It doesn't and shouldn't matter if your partner or parents still support you in anyway at all, or even the reason behind why they do so—the only thing of importance here is your own income.

As you keep that figure in your mind and read through your expenses, take note of how you feel. Because once you start feeling irresponsible as you compare those two figures, your mind will automatically start generating its opinions on the various activities. Do you spend $2 more on super-sizing that burger and don't feel like you need it or could even do without it? Make a note of it next to the space where you recorded that part of your daily expenditure. You spend a lot more on taking a cab home, when the other public transports would suit you just fine? Again, track it next to the spent amounts.

After having gone through every expense in the week, make a weekly total on a separate page. First, concentrate on repeated spending events. So, if you go to your favorite burger place every day, note that and other repetitive expenses down first in the weekly expenditure sheet. Total up the money that you spent on that one activity throughout the week, then read through the weekly expenditure list again after having tallied it all.

For the expenses that you already decided weren't worth it as you were reading through them in the daily columns, mark them on the weekly sheet along with your alternative plan of action. Spend too much on cabs every day and would rather take the bus or train from tomorrow? Mark that up on the weekly sheet. After you've gone through all these expenses, and made a note of the possible changes which you could make that instinctively occurred to you, it's time to pare down other expenses.

This part is going to be much more difficult than the first task. The primary way of cutting down on expenditure to live on less money is by correcting your ignorance of your own spending habits—and that happens to absolutely *everyone* before they learn how to responsibly deal with money. Even people who don't go out partying, stay at home, and make no big splashes, and still find themselves constantly falling short of cash have major areas where improvement and enlightenment of their own proclivities and careless money-related habits would lead to major savings.

However, this second part involves cutting down on stuff which you love. For example, you get together with friends once a week and go to a new restaurant to try out food while hanging out together. However, in this case, you need to ask yourself two questions. The first one is harder to answer—do you make as much money as your friends and can you afford this weekly exercise of spending? If you *do* make as much or more than they do, are your financial objectives the same as theirs? Are they looking for ways to diligently save up their money for a prosperous future as well? If your reply to any of those questions is a no, then you should consider discontinuing this ritual for a time in the future when you'll be able to afford it on a much larger scale, and instead spend time cooking for them or calling everyone to one person's house each week to hang out instead. If the answers to all of those questions was a no, then there's no way around it—you *need* to stop this unnecessary spending and find more cost-effective ways of hanging out with your friends. As dear as your friends as well as this weekly ritual may be to you, and as hard as it may pinch to bring up this topic with them, bankruptcy would hurt you far more.

After first cutting down on expenses of physical convenience or splurging from the first phase of the exercise, and completing the harder task of cutting down expenses of emotional convenience in the second phase, you're now going to come up against the most difficult part of the cost-cutting process in front of you. From within the expenses that *are* left, and which may seem rather skeletal in comparison, you need to figure out how to either drastically reduce your level of necessary expenditure, or at least trim it further down.

Now, more so than convenience, this step hits morale quite drastically. After all, I'm sure you're a hard worker, and the simple truth is that we work harder—regardless of whether we like the job or not—to live a better life, a life of reasonable convenience and luxury, devoid of unnecessary pain and hardships where it can be reasonably helped. However, with rising prices, that's becoming much more difficult to achieve for people with lower incomes or higher financial burdens and responsibilities. As such, when first faced with this phase, people often think of giving up on this process of cost-cutting altogether and just put it off for another time. But, to put it bluntly, such people are morons and will more often than not face crippling financial issues for the rest of their lives till they get in line with this simple fact that you can't have it all, not without grinding your very soul at the altar of your work for quite a long time.

So, if you don't do this voluntarily today, the state of near-poverty will force you to do the same tomorrow. And I promise you, it's much easier to do that with your dignity intact when you're choosing to do so on your own, even if life seems to be pushing you towards that corner anyway. After all, a warrior who steps onto the battlefield voluntarily is far more likely to make it out alive and well than one who is dragged into it unwillingly.

So, if you've managed to reduce your expenses to the bare bones of food, clothing, and shelter, sift through them again to figure out what can be chucked out with minimal difference to your life. And again, having that mind-bogglingly tasty pizza once a week simply to satisfy your taste buds doesn't count as a necessity.

If, like me, you need some good food once in a while to pick up your mood and make the rest of this exercise of saving seem worth it, you can assign yourself a day of the month when you're allowed this above-average indulgence. However, even then, don't lose control and spend enough on that one day to make up the expense side of the column for the whole month. It's still just one day—keep that in perspective. And trust me when I say it's worth it. Once I cut back on a few places which I would hit every month for food, and after I'd dragged myself into financially safer waters, my savings from my favorite pizza place alone accounted for about a tenth of my investment portfolio within that year. Not spending it on all those pizzas led to *many* and *far more delicious* pizzas further down the line.

For a foodie like me, giving up on food expenses while I was building up my wealth was one of the hardest things I ever undertook in my life. But the end result was that I managed to pick up gourmet cooking as a hobby, and I can now make tastier pizzas with the oven that I bought from the profits on investments made from those very pizza savings; it was absolutely worth every moment of sacrifice. And this is just one example out of the hundreds of benefits which you can look forward to in the future once you buckle down on expenditure.

Among these expense lists, and this will become more apparent when looking at the monthly expenses rather than the weekly one, will be the big-ticket items—stuff like your car, rent, etc. Now, and you can only do this if you're serious about a prosperous future, you need to ask yourself really hard questions, such as "Can I afford a place with this high a rent in my situation, or could I rent a cheaper place that would be more sensible, even if it's a bit more inconvenient?" "Do I really need the burden of a car at this point, or could I sell it to create a decent savings amount for myself, while finding other means of transport?"

Moreover, and this precedes every other concern, if you have debts—then those need to be resolved before you even *think* about your own comforts, come what may. Debts are a surefire way of keeping yourself enslaved to the financial credit system, and you're always one mishap away from landing yourself deeper in this quicksand if you miss a single payment for any reason whatsoever. To those people with debts, they're chains around your necks and you need to get rid of them at whatever sacrifice as soon as possible. Otherwise, if you go through a bad patch, it doesn't matter what other efforts you make in life—your house, car, savings, investments, and absolutely any other result of your overall efforts will be in jeopardy if circumstances take a turn for the worse; and they can *always* become worse if you're not well prepared.

Once you've gotten your answers to these hard questions, as well as figured out a way to clear your debt as soon as humanly possible, if you have any, place timelines upon yourself to enact all of them. Every expendable habit which you've identified needs to stop *today*. Not tomorrow, but right now. Because, honestly, that *tomorrow* will never come, and the excuses will never end. Right now, while the motivation behind you taking these steps is still fresh in your mind, you have the highest chance of successfully seeing them through.

In fact, with every half-day that passes between this identification process and the enforcement of the behavioral changes, the chances of you ever implementing and sticking to them drops by another 27%, with people choosing to not implement it at all till circumstances force them once they're past the 2-day mark. After you've identified these necessary changes and implemented them with extreme immediacy, you can't just relax—your battles aren't over yet. In fact, this is *literally* the first step, the absolute beginning of the long-term war of future prosperity vs. short-term convenience.

Chapter 5: Tips for Avoiding Temptation

The point of this chapter is obvious—even if you have the strongest will power on the planet, constant exposure to temptation is simply going to make this journey absolutely miserable for you; you will just end up pushing your morale and energy down, rather than letting you enjoy life more deeply. After all, that *is* the point to achieving independence from material and financial slavery. Again, this doesn't mean you're going to turn yourself into a penny-counting miser, but rather that you'll be in a better position to be able to spend on things which matter most to you. That's because, once you've cut out the expenditures that occur simply because you're too lazy or too careless with your money—the only things that can possibly qualify as valid expenses in that state of mind are ones which matter on a deeper level, such as helping someone in need or getting something really special for someone who deserves it.

So, to make sure that you stick to your prescribed financial diet, you need to act like ex-alcoholics and junkies, and avoid your former spots of spending. This doesn't just mean the exact stores or restaurants that you used to patronize, but rather all others in the same categories and levels of product cost. Instead, explore around for far cheaper alternatives where you can spend your day of indulgence, so that you can get your "hit" of food or shopping without blowing an unnecessary chunk in your monthly budget.

Furthermore, use this as an excuse to inculcate habits which you didn't have before. So, for example, if you're going to a gym—slash the membership fee cost, and instead search for jogging and running routes which would take you along pleasant sceneries every day. Rather than spending time in an air-conditioned gym, the daily exposure and natural exercise would allow you to improve your cardio-vascular fitness while getting you the vitamin D that you need. Essentially, you'd get far more benefits than the gym cost could ever get you, at far lower levels of expense. Also, if you usually indulge in weight training, figure out high-rep exercises to keep your body toned at home instead. Since your weight training would have already increased your core strength, adding stamina and flexibility through home exercises to that regimen would allow you to broach much more varied fields of body-sculpting at far cheaper rates.

Also, stop shopping online altogether. For your food needs, figure out the nearest farmers' markets—they're everywhere—and visit them personally a few times every week in order to get the best produce at cheaper costs. This way—not only would you eat better and healthier, and get fitter as you walk around, but you'll also have the pleasure of forming a personal and regular bond with the sellers who make the very food that you eat. Believe me when I say that having an old farmer's wife who's known you for the past year and can pick out exactly the perfect produce for you from their stall, even before you tell them what you need—just because she deeply wishes to share some of the tastiest ingredients which have come off her farm in the last week—is one of the best feelings you'll ever experience. Plus, platters of food will never taste as good as when they're made from those selective "best ingredients" of the week, at prices which you'd have previously spent on two burger meals and a pack of fries.

Chapter 6: How to Make Use of Automatic Savings

As you must have understood by now, living on the least possible amount of money can only happen when you surround yourself with counter-habits opposing your earlier spendthrift behavior, and by creating enough rituals of smaller and meaningful comfort to see you through this exercise till the point it becomes more ingrained into your personality. Once you're there, it becomes a cake walk. In fact, you begin wondering how you ever managed to go around spending on absurd things, while constantly worrying about money all the time, when there was a much simpler solution always present right before your eyes—stopping yourself from doing just that. However, till you're there, these exercises and behaviors can be a bit of a chore, even when you're financially incapable of spending more. In those moods, saving becomes about survival rather than freedom, and yet again the ability to spend without thinking subconsciously gravitates towards the top of the "future dreams" pile—which is the absolute *opposite* of the point minimalism is trying to teach you.

So, in such cases, a little automatic help to prevent temptation usually goes a long way. To that end, open up another savings account with your bank, and create an automatic monthly transfer that shifts 40% of your income into the new account as soon as your salary gets in. Also, do not take any credit or ATM cards for the new account, and only hang on to a check book. This is to avoid the convenience of being able to swipe a card and spend. Any major monthly expenses which need to happen should first be addressed from your regular account with the 60%. If you happen to need more for any emergency or other such situations, you can go and withdraw that amount alone from the second account.

As this transfer takes place every month, you'll start creating a bit of a nest egg. Also, even though you feel pretty spartan about your expenses after having cut out every bit that you thought you possibly could, the inconvenience of needing to repeatedly go to the bank will ensure that you also cut out any extra bit which could have been removed but hadn't been considered by you because you were hanging on to it for the sake of convenience or empty comfort. Moreover, it will lessen your burden of having to self-discipline as rigorously, as it will create an automatic system where the discipline will be psychologically enforced upon you. Regardless of whichever exercise you choose to do, ensure that you follow through with this one. It's a simple little trick, but an absolute boon to those of us who try to be financially responsible in order to have prosperous futures—and we're a lot that needs every bit of psychological support in achieving this goal that we can get.

Conclusion

Living on less money, or almost no money at all after a point, isn't a difficult objective to achieve in real terms—because the toughest battles that you'll fight will always be with your own mind. However, as I mentioned in the last chapter, every bit of support helps with this goal, so you *need* to share it with your friends and family. Whether you're doing this to survive a bad financial situation or trying to build a base for investment and future wealth, these are noble objectives in today's world of abject greed, and anyone around you who deserves your company *will* understand. They can help by ensuring that they put in effort to avoid places where you'd have to spend too much when together, so that you can still spend as much time as before. Also, if they understand what you're trying to achieve for the sake of your future, they'll also appreciate it more if you put in more effort to keep them happy, rather than money. In such a case, even a humble gift with great personal significance on a birthday can be appropriately appreciated, perhaps more so than an expensive one which took more money than thought to purchase.

Furthermore, in the same vein, savings aren't just about cutting off unnecessary expenditure; they're also about changing the way you look at the world. Therefore, if you can get some money back for recycling your cans and bottles—do that. If you can save wrapping paper for the next time you need to gift someone, put it away for the future.

Also, as a last step, as soon as you reach a stage where you always have some money in the bank—don't just let it stagnate there. Instead, use *strictly* 20% of that amount—no matter how big or small that may be—to research and purchase some shares in respectable and comparatively low risk organizations. There's no better way to appreciate savings than watching that same money grow to many times its original value within a matter of years. Once you reach a stage where you can enjoy that view, you'll have finally placed the last brick in the wall cutting you off from your irresponsible past; because now, if you spend a dollar on any unnecessary purchase, you'll know *exactly* what you could have gotten by investing that dollar instead.

In the end, the most important thing when walking along this path is to let go of the idea that having fewer things around the house somehow makes you worth *less* than you are. *Things* and *stuff* make no difference to the value of a person—it's their personality and character. So, don't become a downer, and figure out cheap or inexpensive hobbies which you can pursue instead to keep your morale high, which you would have never considered otherwise because you were too busy finding new ways to unnecessarily spend your money rather than appreciate everything around you—like trekking, photography, etc.

It's important to find ways to have fun till these behavior patterns are ingrained inside you, since that's all the difference between a miserly penny pincher and a responsible adult who lives on as little money as possible to create financial independence for the future.

Finally, I'd like to thank you for purchasing this book! If you enjoyed it or found it helpful, I'd greatly appreciate it if you'd take a moment to leave a review on Amazon. Thank you!

Printed in Great Britain
by Amazon